So You Know
You're Not Alone

So You Know
You're Not Alone

Becca Taylor

Cover art by Callan Gaines

Edited by Brandon Romain

ISBN (print) 979-8-9913957-7-9
ISBN (eBook) 979-8-9913957-9-3

*to my loving parents
and little brother*

"Be soft. Do not let the world make you hard. Do not let pain make you hate. Do not let the bitterness steal your sweetness. Take pride that even though the rest of the world may disagree, you still believe it to be a beautiful place."
-Kurt Vonnegut, Jr.

"Your heart must become a sea of love,
your mind must become a river of detachment."
-Sri Chinmoy

Thank you for being here,
for opening these pages.

You may not resonate with
everything in them,
that's not what art's about.

The hope is that you find
what does resonate
so you know
you're not alone.

Eternal Sunshine

Once there is human separation, trying to forget
or numb the love is a way humans play safe.

But the scars still remain.

Perhaps in our lifetime,

we are meant to learn the lesson
that each soul we cross paths with
can teach us.

To forget, to avoid the pain
is to miss out on the lesson,
is to miss out on the love.

I get it, I do
the forgetting,
the numbing.

But your soul
came here
to feel it all,

to soar.

And you cannot soar high

and fully appreciate
the beauty, the lightness

without diving into the depths
and feeling that too.

To dive into the depths, is to be free.
Then the fear no longer consumes you,
and you're strong enough to feel it all.

The polarity of this world,
the twisting heartache
mended by precious love.

Dump Out the Poison

Compassion and forgiveness will set you free,
towards others and yourself.

Resentment can cause a block.
Resistance to forgiveness, it harms you.
It doesn't allow your light,
your gifts to shine through.

Have compassion, forgive yourself
and others too
to let yourself freely flow,
shine and share
your beautiful gifts
and creative expression.
It's what you're here to do.

14

It Doesn't Happen for Everyone

With time and awareness,
we awaken to deeper truths.
To age is a beautiful privilege.

In a Moment

The early morning sun rising
over the hill through the Autumn leaves.
A cool warm morning.
Chai latte in hand.
Sweet, warm sips.
Feeling at peace in my heart.
Feeling grateful for the years,
grateful for growth,
grateful to be where I'm at.

My heart whispers:
treasure the moments you feel this way.

Be Easy

Sometimes people have a hard time
wrapping their minds around
who you actually are
and who they want you to be.

Be easy on them.

Love people for who they are.

And when that gets hard,
be easy on yourself too.

Do you avoid your feelings?
Do you press them down?
Do you tell yourself you're
wrong for feeling certain ways?

Be gentle with your feelings.
Hear them out, understand them.
Show them compassion.

Take a few deep breaths.

Can you allow yourself to just feel what you feel?

Is it calling you to create, to move, to pray?

She hears "Go all in, write the ugly."

Yet she still feels resistance to it.
Resistance to admit that life feels hard right now,
That there are many unknowns, a lot of uncertainty.
She has often struggled to accept that,
but has been obsessed with the idea of it.

She thought she was good at accepting uncertainty,
although she realized that she was better at
understanding the concept of the practice.

She thought she demonstrated a cool nonchalance,
but it was a mask.

She pushed down and avoided her feelings so much,
she forgot that it was a mask she was wearing.

Her thoughts shift and she remembers
that there is certainty in this world.
Certainty of goodness, certainty of her soul's calling,
certainty of love and of God's plan.

This helps her to trust in
the best possible outcome,
in the highest good for all.

Your moods and thoughts will shift.
Move with them. Surrender.

Live the life
you are meant to live.

May the sunshine fuel
peace and trust in your heart
for all that is meant for you.

To feel so deeply.
The highs, the lows.

Thoughts and feelings
are literally addicting.

Be mindful of this.

And numbing the feelings, still
fuels what is producing them.

You can try to dull them out,
but the real cure is to

feel and
let it go.

Change is coming,
as it always is.

But sometimes
it just feels different,
bigger.

Like it's right around the corner
and you're scared to look.

It's what you've been wanting
but you don't want to let go
of where you're at.

Just keep creeping towards that corner.

Be brave and leave the past behind

so, you can taste the beautiful future

that's been seeking you.

Can you just show up
without the need to try to prove yourself?
Can you just show up with your mess?

Without the choking desire
to share all that's going well in your life?
Or the thought of hiding if your life
isn't everything you want it to be just yet?

As if reaching your milestones that you created
in your own head would help you feel
more accepted, more liked, more welcome?

The people who desire to deeply connect
are not focused on
the money you're making,
how clean your apartment is,
if you're in a relationship.

They just care that
you are
happy.

They just care that
you feel genuine love
in your heart.

the beauty of this world
the cotton candy sky
wispy colorful clouds
as the sun sets
and the crescent moon hangs.

a turtle swims in the water
dips down, comes back up,
and dips down again.

I walk forward,
heart feeling so full
of joy from the beauty
and magic of existence.

a falcon flies across the
road in front of me
and lands on a branch.

I keep walking
and see an intricate
bird's nest on the ground,
so perfectly made.

and then there is a large frog
in the middle of the road.

I get behind it so it
hop, hop, hops
to safety; shortly after
a car drives by

and I pick up my phone,
keep walking
and write this while

dusk approaches
and fireflies, flicker.

You're strong to be soft

after feeling hurt.

You're brave to keep loving.
To laugh, to play.

You're meant to learn from where you're at,
from what you're feeling, right now.

It's okay to just let yourself feel it,
to be okay with being uncomfortable.

When you feel it,
you transmute it,

instead of stuffing it deeper into the subconscious
and letting it run the show.

It rained today,
inside of me and
the fog hung heavy
against the mossy
dead tree forest.

Explanation after explanation.
Words and more words.
Trying to prove something.

But the best thing
at times
can truly be,
to just be.

To relax and
settle into the now.

To feel gratitude for this life,
letting it flow, ever so sweet.

Space to Relax

You can never truly know
what another is thinking.

Give yourself a moment
to tune into what is real within you
rather than your perception of others.

Let go of the stories you've created
about what others *may* be thinking
so you can be joyful,
so you can be free.

Self-Destructive Thoughts

Thinking of revenge but
instead I choose to

forgive,
forgive,
forgive,

so I can be free,
so I can breathe easy.

I ask my ego,
"what's the reason
for the anger?
What do you want,
what is your purpose?

"To feel loved,"
it cries.

"Do you realize that what you're doing will bring the
opposite?"

"I want to push others away so I can't feel neglected."

"But then you will feel just that."

It cries again.

"How about we just let our self, love?
How about we accept that we may feel heartache?
But know that the love we are blessed with
in this lifetime, is more than worth it."

Comfort washes over, and the ego
decides to let go
and trust.

It's okay to be scared,
let yourself feel it,
but don't let it consume you

Let it go, let it go.

Allow yourself
to experience
love in
your one
precious life.

The fear of being alone
cuts so deep.

We just want love,
we want safety, security,
to be told we did a good job.

Be gentle with yourself
when the panic sets in,
when the waiting comes
and you feel uncomfortable
in your own company.

Hug your own arms,
let yourself know:

I got you.

Let yourself feel it all and know
we all have similar feelings,
similar fears, the desire for love.

Fill others hearts with the
love you desire, and your
heart will be full, too.

Feel the barriers slip away,
feel the fear dissipate.

Triggers can lead to feeling separate.
The trick is to ask yourself in those moments,
How can I come back to love?
How can I soften my heart?

Rather than pull away
and close off,
lean in closer.

There is beauty on the other side.

Dear Ego,

I know you love to blame and separate.
I know it helps you feel safe.
I know your intention is to protect me,
but can you also see how this brings me further from love
and a deeper learning about true connection?

I deeply thank you for trying to protect me,
but how would it feel if we leaned deeper
into love and allowed ourselves to be
open to feeling all that comes with it?

The joy, the sadness, the vulnerability?

Through it all, we could make some art?
Maybe write some books?

When we try to control the outcome,
we're not open to the beautiful
synchronicities life and love have to offer.

How about we soften our heart and surrender?
Surrender to being so deeply held?
Surrender to being vulnerable, to sharing
our inner world, to relating to others
and forming genuine connection?

Love Always,
Your Loving Self

33

We're all different.
No better or worse than the next.
We just are.

Different ways of processing information.
Your way is not the only right way.

I remember watching a roommate in college
put dressing on their salad a different way than I did
and thinking "that's not the way you do it."
I think I even suggested they do it another way.

But that is how they do it,
and my way is not the only way,
and it's not the "right" way.

Your way is not the only way,
but it is the way meant for you.

Another's way is not better than your own.

What works for you?

What is unique to you?

In what ways can you be
more accepting of both
yourself and others?

34

I was living each day like I had a million more to live.

Avoiding connection as if I'd ever
see that person again in their current state of being.

I sat and stared over the lake
as a toddler and her mother approached,
the toddler calling out to the ducks,
a brief conversation.
When I was a kid
my parents took me to see the geese.
I loved saying "duck".

Then I passed a woman with her mother,
now in a wheelchair, and
a teenaged boy and girl on a swing set.

Two women with a man in a wheelchair
with a little dachshund puppy.
I asked to pet it, joy and excitement filling my heart.
I had a mini dachshund growing up.

This beautiful temporary existence.

I was acting as if I'd have a million more days.

But as I walked from the lake

I felt how deeply precious this one moment truly is.

Just being here, tears welling up.

To love and be loved
while we are here.

How delicate and
beautiful to be
in the midst of it all.

Allow Peace to Reveal Itself

Let us be patient with ourselves,
with our moods, our thoughts,
and understand that they shift.

To be patient,
to not take anything too seriously,
and know our thoughts
are not always true.

To allow our emotions to flow
and know we can
manage how we respond
to our moods,
to our thoughts.

It is not always about control
of the outside,
nor the inside,

rather how we respond
to them both.

Psalm Thirty Four Eighteen

I remember being very young, maybe 8,
laying at the end of the bed that pulled out of the sofa,
watching a movie with family, lights dim.

Tucked in the caved in space of mattress
between the bottom and middle bars.

I remember pretending
to have a broken heart,
romanticizing it.

Today, I wonder what that says about my soul,
about my choices.

That little me, perhaps she knows more than I do.

The inevitable pain that accompanies being human.

Chaos turned to art.

Embracing blank canvases.

Detach from the idea
that you need to be happy
by stuff that doesn't actually
make you happy.

Listen to your
heart's song
and share it.

What lights you up?

What do you feel in your core
you're here to share with
those meant to hear it?

Speak up
so they can
hear you.

When it comes to love,
I'm obsessed and scared.

A terrified romantic.

Once given the love I desire,
my brain questions if its real,
or if I deserve it.

Then I remember that

life is allowed to feel really good,
life is allowed to be abundant,
free and full of ease.

Life is allowed to be full of
genuine love.

Your voice is unique.

Trust the message
you're here to share.

You are powerful.

Own your voice,
use your voice.

You do not have to water yourself down
to be accepted, to be loved.

The vulnerable you
is deeply loved.
Don't you feel that?

Do not allow your own thoughts,
your own fears of
what others may think
to hold you back.

Your perception is a narrative.

Whatever story you're telling yourself
becomes true to you.

Your mind will look for ways to prove what you tell it,
so be careful what you feed your mind with.

How can you shift the narrative
in your brain to serve yourself
and others?

Grasping for moments.
Missing them as soon as they're gone.
Worried about having missed something.
Being grateful for every hug exchanged.

"I'm having fun,"
I think.
So I take a sip
and take another.

But what am I really hiding?
That aging scares me?
That I miss younger years?
Or maybe just the idea of them.

At 12, I remember laying in bed
crying and crying.

I knew I was growing up and
there was nothing I could do about it.

I think that little girl re-surfaced last night.
Wanting to stay at the family Christmas party,
holding on just a bit longer.

Crying a bit, thinking of
how much has changed
and how people and things
don't always turn out in the
picturesque way you thought
they may and that that's okay.

My sensitive mind may miss the past,
be scared of the future, and
forget to be present sometimes.

But that's okay.
I still love my mind,
dearly.

My heart says be still,
we've got this.
I am so, so proud of you.

Let yourself feel anger, sadness.
Dance it out, write it out.
Catharsis. Pray, pray, pray.
What creative outlet transmutes
the fear to peace?

In peace, your light shines.
In peace, you share your message with clarity.
Feel what you feel.
Honor your feelings.
Be gentle and understanding towards yourself.

Be curious,
compassionate.

Rage may rise.
This human life is full
of reasons to feel it.

But you can re-frame the thoughts
after expressing the emotion.

Then I have compassion towards myself.
What am I longing for?
How can I get there?
I hear you, I hear you.

This mood will shift,
as they always do.

Be patient,
be loving,
be kind.

I feel deeply.
So, I keep writing,
breathing deep,
stretching
and practicing
intentional thought.

Your life is a masterpiece
and art, it's never perfect.

It's not supposed to be.

It's Okay to Be Sad

Acknowledge your feelings,
acknowledge the part of you
that feels what it feels.

When you push part of yourself away,
it creates a feeling of shame.

When you invite that part of you in,
and give it space to be heard
healing begins.

No more "oh, I'm fine" –

more compassion,
more curiosity

for the part of you
that just wants
to be
heard.

Write, sing, paint,
express your emotions.

Make your life
a moving piece of art.

And pray,
always remember to pray.

Sink into the eternity of time and know
there is nowhere you "have" to be,
you have arrived.

Focus on the people
who love you,
who cheer you on.

Don't fall for those
sneaky thoughts that doubt
they're being genuine.

Receive the love,
feel the love,
and let it warm you.

The change is coming.

Settle into the stillness
of your new vibration.

The freedom
is here now.
Be excited.

Imagine waking up every day,
living the life you dream of.

How does it feel?

Take a moment,
be still

and breathe in
that feeling.

Have you ever
taken a moment
to breathe in
and sit in the stillness
of how living the life you desire,
living the life,
you're meant to live,
truly feels?

Keep sitting in that feeling,
and you will wake up
and see it was never about
getting where you wanted,
rather it was about shifting
your mental state to be
so deeply grateful with
this life you have been gifted.

And once that feeling arrives,
keep accessing it, day after day.

The lifestyle you're seeking
is all in your mindset.

Release Control

Act with a gentle ease.
Step by step, without demanding
an immediate outcome.

What is meant to be will flow to you.
Keep taking it step by step.

You'll look back at the journey
with peace and gratitude
in your heart, marveling
at how far you've come.

Instead of existing in a state
of "more, more! not enough!"

Exist in a state of gratitude,
where you're so content with
where you're at, knowing blessings
are on their way.

Slow down.

Let the thoughts come
and go.

Return to the space within.

The space that knows no time.

That space that knows
this moment, right now
is enough.

Be gentle, be easy and
be understanding with yourself.
Shame is ineffective.

Loosen your grip.

Show yourself love.

The work you feel called to do, matters.
The voice within you, matters.

The message you feel swirling within you, matters.

It is unique to you.

Only you can share your gifts the way you can.

Your thoughts can be based in gratitude or lack,
in being present or wanting to be elsewhere.

To feel grateful and present in this life

reframe your thoughts
so you may deeply enjoy
the moment in front of you,
and all you've been gifted.

Reframe your thoughts to focus on gratitude,
to focus on the present moment.

What you choose to focus on,
grows in your perception.

You're Most Like You

So often I think we are compared to
parents, grandparents, aunts, uncles,
anyone who raised us.

Of course, we pick up habits, behaviors, beliefs,
that is just how the subconscious works.

But at the end of the day,
you are always most like you
and the space within.

It's your choice to break the patterns
you picked up from childhood.

It's your choice to break a certain belief.

It's your choice to become
closer to your true essence.

Rather than listen to outside voices that try to define you
and tell you who you are. You already know who you are.

Don't let the outside voices get in your head.

You get to define yourself.

It is your choice to listen to
the voices and allow yourself
to become that person.

Realize that your
true nature is your soul.
Get closer to that.

You will always be
most like you.

You are the only person
who can do what you do,
the way that you do it.

Once you truly feel that,
there is no room for comparison,
no room for insecurity.

57

To cope with the fear,
the uncertainty,
focus on your faith.

Focus on the infinite space within you,
that knows God has a plan for you,
that knows He is guiding you.

Let go of fear and trust.

Enjoy the ride,
and pray.

Always, always pray.

We get so wrapped up in our future plans,
worried they won't turn out exactly the way we dream.

Well, they may not turn out exactly that way,
but that doesn't mean they won't turn out better.

Be here now, have gratitude for where you are at now,
connect to God and the inner space within you each day,
and let that lead the way.

We all
have wounds
we are healing.

Be kind,
and drop the
assumptions
of others.

This morning, I told myself
"you're beautiful"
and tears unexpectedly
began rolling down my cheeks.

Why do so many of us
wait for another to tell us so?

Why do we question
our own beauty?
And connect it
to our worthiness?

You are beautiful
because you are here,
because you exist.

You are the only you.

Sing your song, the way
only you can.

You are inherently
beautiful.

You are who
you are meant to be.

How can you deeply
embrace your uniqueness?

Look within
for inspiration.

For if you look without,
your authenticity
will become lifeless.

For when you look within,
you evoke pure interest.

Because we all on some level
wish to deeply know ourselves
and when you do so
you mirror that possibility to another.

You show them the possibility
of authenticity for their self.

When you look without for approval
and waste your authenticity,
you feel unaligned.

Stop focusing so much on others
and turn your gaze within.

Release It

Instead of mentally obsessing
on the negative feeling,

turn it in into art.

By tapping into your creative essence,
you tap into your true essence
and see that this is what
the negative ego is trying to do
when it focuses on the feeling.

However, the negative ego's behavior often
attracts the opposite of what it actually wants.

Until you bring awareness to it,
and help it see that there is a
more creative, effective way.

So many of us
want to be
liked,
admired,
respected.

To become pure of heart,
to deeply love,
is to take down the barriers
of being separate and
rid the feeling
of wanting
to be "better than."

We want a neat,
little buttoned up ending,
you know?

But that is not real.

There's more story
to the "happily ever after."

There's diving deep,
there is healing,
there is unlearning
all that holds us back.

Hold Onto It

Listen to God,
listen to your inner voice,
not everyone else's.

Hold the vision.
Hold the vision.
Hold the vision.

Trust in the plan.
Be patient.

Reflect on how
far you've come.

You're allowed to take up space.
You're allowed to share your voice.
You're allowed to make yourself seen.

You are a powerful human.

Share your art,
share your uniqueness.

Do the things that
when you look back,
you're grateful you did.

Be gentle with yourself.
Be gentle with your thoughts.
Release shame, release guilt.

Allow yourself to be
with the discomfort,
feel it to heal it.

Breathe and focus on your breath.

Be in this one moment.

Forgive yourself.
Be here now.
Breathe into the moment.

You are a beautiful being, choose love.
What is something you can do in this moment,
to make yourself feel more comfortable,
to make yourself feel more loved?

You know in your soul
you're meant for that thing
you can't stop thinking of.

So, what's holding you back
from just going for it?

Focus on your vision.

Use your pain as fuel
to focus on your mission.

Often our deepest struggles
point the way
to what we're here to learn
and overcome in this life.

The pain is not be avoided,
nor given control.

It is to be transmuted
to art, to service.

We are not separate in our pain.

It is a part of the human experience.

But beneath the pain, is love.

May you find the strength
to transmute the pain to love.

Embrace the discomfort.

You are an artist.

You are here to deeply
experience this life.

So let it flow through you.

Embrace the highs, the lows.

I know you feel them both so deeply.

Let life flow through you,
wash over you,
drag you into the sea
and land you back at the shore,
returning with more
trust in the journey,

in God,
in yourself,
than ever before.

You aren't meant to remain in the shallows.

You are meant to go deep.

Deep
Deep
Deep

So let it flow through you.
The highs, the lows,
all of it.

You are an artist.

You are human.

This human experience
can be felt
so deeply
if you allow it.

Let it flow through you,
and remember to always,
always come back to love.

If you feel you are meant to create,
give yourself space to be still,
to be silent.

I mean, I think everyone
could benefit from stillness,
from silence.

But I truly believe that creation arises
when you make space for it.

Beware a full calendar,
beware not giving yourself
time and space to just be.

Fill up your cup before
filling up others.

Set boundaries
to come home
to the space within,

to make space to
allow the ideas
to bubble up
and spill out of you.

To Flow

To live in what makes your soul sing.
To feel love, to feel warmth, to just feel.
Towards humans, animals, plants.
To live with compassion.
To gently follow what softly
pulls you towards it.

To be present. To be mindful.
To let go of all expectations and exist in this one moment.
To enjoy fully. To let go of questions. To let go of fear.

To show up as you are
and allow yourself to just be.
Repeat that, "to just be."

To let what may arise, do so.
To do what feels aligned for you.
To stay grounded, rooted, calm.

Surrender

It's okay to not be okay.
Can you allow yourself
to just be with it?

You are human.
Be easy on yourself.

Do something small, every day
towards your vision.

If not every day, most,
to keep the momentum.

And if you slip up
give yourself grace.
Taking a break is okay,
just get back to it.

Find peace in the journey.

Learning to be still between
the happiness, the sadness.

Learning to silence the mind in the chaos.
So that it may remain inspired instead of frightened.

To feel the soul dance within
this terribly temporary, inexplicable,
painfully beautiful existence.

I laughed
and looked up,
out of the
coffee shop
window.

Four hawks
flew, circular
beneath the moon
in blue daylight.
And I felt magnetism
to the core.

Confusion will find you
and it will leave.
You may feel hurt,
you may feel guilt.
And being human,
it can eat you up.

But if you keep going and
you choose love,
you choose joy,
you choose freedom

you'll feel like
one of the lucky ones
that got out alive.

Everyone has that power,
to choose how to react to
what goes on within.

Don't succumb
to the emotions
that drain you.

Find stillness,
breathe deep
into your heart,
into your mind.
Find lightness
and carry that
with you.

Nothing is ever what it seems.

Thoughts don't match the "real" world.

They are their own world,
you are your own galaxy.

And there are billions
of other galaxies
moving differently
than your own.

To sing and dance and laugh.
To follow the soul.
To trust in goodness.

To feel the sunshine,
hear the birds chirp.

These things I am grateful for.

Grateful to trust,
grateful for grace.

To follow the steady pull

to help others,
live simply,
love, always.

Always love.

Nature doesn't rush,
nature doesn't worry.

The dewy grass,
the yellow dandelions
surrounded by so much green.
The weeds, the daisies.
The delicate little daisies.

They grow at their own pace
and no one gets mad
at them or impatient.

The beauty, to marvel at and to breathe it in.
To appreciate the impermanence of it all.
This magnificent world of ours, its own pace.

Instead of trying to change it
or beg from it, stability,
why not just enjoy what we can?

To just breathe and love all
of its beauty for what it is
and where it's at?

Including ourselves.

We are meant to learn
to adjust our sails
with every change
in the current,
in the wind.

I'm afraid if we don't
we will cause more frustration,
more disappointment
opposed to if we simply
surrender.

To rebel is to be so very free
that your entire existence
is acceptance, is flow.

To age is to scar.
One cannot live in this world without one.
To run about fearing hurt,
fearing change is useless.
Allowing that fear
to dictate our state of being
– futile.

We can hold onto our hopes and dreams.
We can kick and scream,
forcing them into our lives.
Or we can simply, be.

Work toward those goals of course,
with a sense of knowing that
what is meant to be is on its way to you.

And trust that all is happening
as it is meant to happen.

Even if your stomach churns,
your palms get sweaty,
your heart hurts and
nothing seems to make sense.

Allow yourself to be with what is
and trust that one day it will.

Trust that it's true,

we would not know light
without a little bit of darkness.

But I'll tell you a secret;
the light always wins.

I think one of the greatest gifts
we can give to ourselves
is power over our own thoughts
and awareness that
not everything we think is true.

Our reaction to our thoughts
is what we truly have control over.
Our reaction to our perception
is everything.

We can feed our head
with the need for
power and control
over things surrounding us
and we will most likely find
ourselves disappointed.

We cannot expect
to control the outside world.
But what we can do,
is practice surrender,
practice detachment and
find ourselves in flow.

When we let go,
when we allow things exterior to us to just be
we can become inspired by what surrounds us.

That is when we can choose
to focus on the magical moments,
those moments where we feel
deep gratitude.

This does not mean perfection
and it does not mean always feeling good.
To me, it means patience, in everything.

It means understanding
that what truly belongs
in your life, will be in it.

Patience

Allow growth to happen gradually.
Strong foundations are incredibly important.

Be patient enough to allow your feelings to flow.
Feel the feelings and know you
can control your reaction to them.

To not be in a rush,
to truly slow down,
to follow your intuition
and listen to your inner teacher.`

To truly take care of yourself.
To listen to your mind, to your heart,
to your body, to your soul.

Tune in, have an awareness.

Be patient while getting to know yourself, too.

I think it may take a lifetime.

There is a raging fire
that burns within me.

Some days I feel them more than others,
and it keeps me inspired.

We all got that magic within us.

Let yourself feel it.
Let yourself feel it.

I cried today, fearful of
change. Frightened
by growth.

I've been so committed to my growth,
so stoked on it.

I think it's only normal to feel fear,
to want to retreat back to an old self.

Can you relate?

I let myself feel the sadness,
then I released it and moved on.
Grasping at moments, things,
even versions of self can cause
more discomfort than the letting go does.

Let us flow, let us give ourselves room to breathe.
To shift, to bloom, and to embrace
the moments of our lives as they unfold.

As my mom always says,
"You just have to enjoy every stage of life"

"The soul always knows what to do to heal itself.
The challenge is to silence the mind." -Caroline Myss

Yesterday was a good day
to feel the warm breeze
on your bare arms.

The sunshine on your face
streaming through the trees
as you step throughout the
freshly green forest.

To smell the coolness,
and hear the rumble
of running water.

To feel calm,
to feel peace
and be still.

To let your mind rest,
breathe deep

and just be.

Forgive yourself.

Release yourself from
the negative narrative
you've written in your head.

Release yourself from the guilt.

Love yourself deeply,
and become so very free.

Do you have dreams?

Do you have moments
in life where you know
you can accomplish
what you are truly meant for
and set your mind and actions to?

Do you feel it in your soul?

Are these moments often
followed by periods of self-doubt?

Yeah, I get that too.

But here's the thing.

Whatever you keep telling yourself,
whatever thoughts you continually think,
you will keep perceiving as true.

I'm going to tell you a little secret though.

The fact that you can do
what you are called to do
is way, way more true.

Really tap into that feeling.

Feel scared and do it anyway.

Step into even more action
when you start to doubt yourself.

Keep believing in
and acting
on those
dreams.

You Are Expansive

Crush your self-limiting beliefs by
doing the thing you say you are going to do.

Learn to cultivate a deep trust within yourself.

Do these things now and tomorrow and the day after.

Do these things because
you are worthy
of the love
and the life
that you desire.

Trust your intuition.
Trust that you are being guided.

Trust in Divine timing.

Listen to your inner voice,
listen to the inner teacher,
the slight nudges.

When your heart speaks
and says do this or no, don't do that.

The more you trust
the more you see that
miracles happen,
all the time.

Miracles are the natural way
in which God operates.

Imagine a life in which you allowed yourself to trust that
everything is happening not *to* you, but *for* you.

Accept and forgive so that you may find peace.
Accept and forgive so you can move past resentment,
so you can let go of the heaviness in your heart.

Allow yourself to shine your light,
to settle into peace and clarity.

Allow yourself to flow within the state truest to you,
so that you may embody your most authentic self.

That person you envision yourself to be.

How do they vibrate?
What are their thoughts?
What do they spend their time doing?
Are they tapping into their creativity?

Can you start tuning into
that way of being,
today?

Gratitude

Listen, if you cannot allow yourself
to see and feel grateful for what
you already have,
it will never feel like
you have enough.

But when you allow yourself
to truly see what you have and
FEEL gratitude for it,

you live in a state of abundance.

The stories you've created in your head
will keep coming up for you until you allow yourself
to become an observer of your thoughts
rather than picking at them and letting them control you.

The stories you've created in your head
will keep coming up for you until you
dig below the surface and
figure out the reason they are there.

Allow yourself to feel
what they make you feel
and release them,
because they no longer serve you.

These stories you have made up
because you subconsciously feel
you are unworthy of believing
good things for yourself.

(and give yourself time to heal the stories,
be patient with yourself)

They still may come up
when you think they were done with,

like the red from a pimple healing
on your face you wish you didn't touch.

It might not heal tomorrow
or the next day,
but eventually it will

and next time you'll resist the urge
to touch your face.

(like you resist the urge
to create the negative story)

To develop a deep relationship with yourself,
you must know how
worthy you are
of experiencing a blissful life.

Dear Empath

You're meant to
make time to

rest, to re-store,

to do what you really love to do.

Set boundaries for yourself.

Move your body.
Stretch, dance, walk,
so you can move
through your emotions.

Make time to meditate.

Limit recreational social media
browsing and news exposure.

Perhaps at times the first hour
of your morning
is away from
bright lights,
the phone,
and others.

I believe everyone
has something that feels good for them,
but if this feels good for you,

give that first bit of your day
to really connect with yourself.

Be protective
of yourself
and your time.

Embrace environments
that nourish you.

It's not selfish,
because when you find

what truly nourishes you
and allow it to do so,
you are then able to give
to the world
your most authentic self.

When you allow yourself
to step into your most authentic self,
you inspire others to do the same.

Fear and jealousy
keep you small.

Harmonize with the ego,
that thinks fears and jealousies
are so, so big.

I understand,
I get it,
I feel those things too.

Expand into yourself,
into your soul and
watch the space
they take up in your life,
fade away.

Know you are a unique being,
who, when follows the path
of the highest good,
has nothing to fear,
nothing to envy.

To the fears your mind creates,
your soul knows the way.

To the jealousy you feel of others,
your soul knows how magnificently
unique you truly are.

Expand into that,

trust it.

Change

We fear change.
We avoid change.

We allow ourselves
to be uncomfortable
so that we remain
"comfortable."

Thoughts and feelings
are addicting.
Even if they are
thoughts and feelings
you don't particularly enjoy.

When shedding what is
not meant for you,
be patient with the process.

Making space for joy,
for freedom is always
worth it.

The discomfort in between
is part of the journey.

Allow yourself to feel
what it is that you feel.

The other side is
waiting, patiently
seeking you.

Make space to be silent.
Make space to be still.
Make space to pray.
Make space to truly connect
to the space within.

My worried thoughts often come
when paying too much mind
to the exterior world and
trying to control it.

Trust that you
are doing enough.

Trust that God is
preparing something
beautiful for you.

Stop looking for answers
in social media.

Inner peace, happiness,
and freedom are available
to you now.

Take time to find
what you truly love.

I've found for me,
it's about stripping
back ideas about who
I think I "should" be
and settling into what
truly resonates
with my soul.

I feel unsettled
but then I put
the pen to paper.

It all fades away
and all that exists
is the art.

The ink, the words,
healing my soul.

Make space for what
elevates your heart.

Focus on getting
into that element.

Allow yourself to
relax into that feeling.

When you allow yourself to
really be in that feeling,
you'll attract more of that into your life.

What you focus on, grows.

If the art is within you,
the art is within you.

There is nothing you
must do to draw it out.
Rather, it is what
you must *not* do.

In the silence, the stillness, the being,
you make space for the art to come
through you.

Your art is not something
that only existed in your past.
Nor some abstract future idea you'll get to.
If it was within you, it is still within you.
If you believe it will come through in the future,
it can come through now.

It will always be.

Trust that it is always on its way to you.
Make time to be still, to not grasp too hard,
to make time to allow yourself
to really hear it.

You wanted change
for so long, but
you feared it.

Now, you're past that
and you're diving
deep - you're healing.

You've chosen to live
the life you're meant for.

Relax, breathe deep and release.

Know this is all happening *for* you.
Can you soften into that?
Can you find peace in
the journey of where you think
you're "supposed" to go?

Allow yourself
to trust and pray,
knowing everything
will be okay.

Let yourself be
all the way alive.

Let the fear,
the excitement
wash over you.

Love others, do good
and pray, God is always
with you on the journey.

Let go and let yourself be led.

Listen to God
and your
inner knowing.

Rid yourself of all that does not serve you
and see your life fill with what is meant for you.

Reframe your Thoughts, Trust

Your thoughts can be based in gratitude or lack,
in presence or wanting to be elsewhere.

Enjoy life.
Feel gratitude.
Be present.

Pray and allow God's plan
to unfold.

Because it is better than anything
you could imagine.

To calm the waters within,
to breathe, to connect to
the space within.
To connect to God
and truly trust

miracles are
the natural way.

I'm Trying to Believe This Myself

You're as unique and
expansive as the night sky.

Don't wish anything
about you different.

You are perfect

as you are.

In a dark moment
remind yourself
how powerful
you truly are.

Remind yourself
how Divinely
held you are.

This is just
the beginning.

The moment will come
when the sun starts
to peak above the horizon

and gold light
will flicker about
your heart.

If You Want Expansion

Cherish the moments
in your days,
even if it's just a moment,
that feels how you desire
life to always feel.

What you focus on,
expands.

This life is too precious to
stay on the sidelines,

to only use the same
machines at the gym,
to never book the trip.

To be free is
a mindset.

You choose to experience
the new

or you stay "safe"
in what you know.

Does your heart swell
in your current state of mind,
with your current choices?

It may feel uncomfortable at first
to choose the things
you normally don't.

The brain resists change,
but you'll prove to yourself
that change is safe.

Expand into your being.

The thing about your dream is,
it's not meant to happen overnight.

It takes planting a seed and watering it.

At times perhaps, being okay with
when that seed does not sprout
and having the courage to
plant another.

Tenderly caring to them with
love, devotion, and patience.

You Can't Force It

You can't force the words to flow through.
You can't force yourself to be someone you're not.
You can't force yourself to be happy.

What you can do is
let the thoughts,
the feelings,
pass through you
without attaching
too much meaning.

So the words,
yourself,
happiness,

naturally reveal
their selves.

A Sensitive Soul

At times, she felt
too sensitive
for this world.

Like when she dug below
the surface, she'd realized
a piece of her was
always grieving.

She was anxious all day,
and once she allowed
her mind to rest
she realized she was
at a wake last night

for a childhood friend's dad.
Memories of silly teenage
years bubble up.

Those careless days
when you don't deeply
realize that this really
doesn't
last forever.

A part of her grieves for
the boy who sat in front of her
in junior year high school class,
who one day left that seat
empty.

A part of her grieves for the boy in middle school
that cried as he shared with the class that
his hamster died in his hands
and asked if anyone knew how it felt,
to know that you can't do anything about it.

She realizes that a piece of her brain
covers these feelings up with
anger, avoidance, distraction

and when she feels them,
they hit too deep.

I Wonder

I wonder what that poem said,
the one I had in my head
then forgot before
I became alone with a pen.

Speak up,
even if your
hands sweat.

When the words bubble up,
allow them to spill.

Your words make an impact.

Breathe deep,
and feel that.

We think the
next moment
will be "better."

We think somehow
we'll be happy then,
in some foreign time.

But happiness
comes from shifting
your mindset
in the moment.

If you knew the depth
of everyone's story,
I suspect you'd be
a bit more gentle.

One of the bravest
things you can do
is gracefully let go
of people, places, things
no longer meant for you.

Life is real
and it's raw.

Things happen
that we don't
particularly
want to happen.
But they do,
that's just life.

You're strong enough
to be with what
is happening.

As the saying goes,
this too shall pass.

Be with the
sweet moments, too.

That moment in the snow.

The one where
it's late and the snowflakes
are swirling about,
streetlights illuminating
the dancing flurries.

You stick your tongue out
and taste what it was like
to be a kid, eating snow
without a care in the world.

Healthy Independence

Being with
another
does not make you
someone.

You are always
someone
with or without
another.

Forgive

Guilt is
inevitable.

You choose
to sit in it
or forgive
yourself
for being
human.

You are
not trapped.

You have
choices.

What it may take,
is uncomfortable action.

Next time you find
yourself
feeling trapped
ask yourself,

*am I just scared
of what would
set me free?*

Everybody is
somebody.

We all have
our own special
internal world.

Remember that
the things outside of you
are not you.

The clothes,
the furniture,
the things you feel
so attached to
are not *you*.

When you feel down
about your art,
when you doubt yourself,
don't give up.

It's a part of the process,
sometimes it's just a mood.

Go back to your project the next day,
without such a forced feeling
but with a flow sense,

appreciating the messages
that come through you.

In the mornings
with myself,

the sunshine,
a warm drink,
a notebook,
a pen,

my thoughts,
my feelings,
and prayers.

I am happy,
I am free.

No one can convince you a thing.
It is up to you to make a choice
and include it in your life.

I sit at the beach
thinking and feeling the thought,
"I am so grateful for this life."

It is 5:03pm,
not yet golden hour
but nearly there.

Earlier I had a swim,
went for a walk.

A seagull caws,
another glides
over the wet sand.

People talk and wander
along the water's edge.
Kids play, people swim,
sailboats breeze in the distance.

Blue sky, sand, dark blue water,
puffy white clouds paint
a beautiful sight.

Evenings at the beach
fill my heart and soul
with such peace and joy.

I go to grab my pen
but don't have one.

So I open my phone notes,
to encapsulate
this moment.

Breathing into my heart, finding eternity
in this one simple, intricate moment.

It's okay to feel
nostalgia
towards the past,
but let it pass.

How can you
bring that feeling
you're remembering
into the present?

It's okay to have fear and doubt.
Move through them, keep going.
Stay true to your passions.

You will end up where
you are meant to be.

You have no idea
how wildly beautiful
your destination is.

You have no idea the
wild synchronicities
that will happen
along the way.

You have no idea
how it's going to happen.

Just know, your destination
is happiness

so just have fun
along the way.

Be like the plant
that kept growing
because it was moved
to a more spacious pot.

Move past discomfort,
delight*fully* bloom.

Don't Abandon Yourself

When you're feeling off
be with yourself,
be with your feelings
let yourself process it.

Your moments aren't ruined
just because you aren't
feeling your best.

You can still find comfort
in the moments your emotions
aren't so desirable.

Let yourself know,
"I got you, I understand,
it's okay you feel this way,
I'm not going anywhere"
and let yourself feel it,
to shift it.

Your mind may shift,
and thoughts feel heavy.
Confusion may set in.

But remember:
your thoughts are not you,
your feelings are not you.

Take a deep breath.

Be still and know
that you are held.

Be still and breathe
to find calm,
to move
forward.

Through Murky Waters, We Bloom

Let the emotions flow through you,
and return to the stillness within.

Surrender to the feelings
to transmute them.

Don't try to force a different feeling.

Just acknowledge the thoughts
and feelings that are coming up.

Don't attach too much meaning to them.

Let them come and let them go.

It's okay
to change,
shift and
evolve.

Stop thinking
you're not
doing something
"good" enough.

Give yourself credit
for taking the time
and having courage
to show up and do
what you have done.

This Is Where I Desire to Be

Evenings by the sea,
pen and notebook near
spa days, hot tub nights,
dancing beneath the stars
pouring my full heart
onto the page
sharing it
with you.

I am so grateful
for the gifts
I've been given
and get to
work with
in this
precious life.

Show love
to all parts,
to all versions
of yourself.

Prayer,
patience,
trust –

ingredients
for clarity.

I can never
know the future.

I cannot predict
the when
or the how.

But I can
find comfort
in trusting God
to guide me

and know
His timing
is perfect.

Create a mindset
that feels like art.

One where you
don't demand perfection

but find the perfect
within what is

and appreciate the beauty,

appreciate the feeling
of where you're at.

I think the reason that
at times I've felt
lost and heartbroken -

I kept putting
my relationship
with things
outside of me

before relationship
with my self

and with God.

Stop saying yes
to everything
because you feel like
you "have" to.

You don't *have* to have
kids or a
mortgage or a
marriage.

You also don't *not* have
to have these things.

Trust what you are
called towards
in this one
precious life.

You've just got to do what
you feel called to do.

Choose to show up.

Embrace the edge
and be okay with
the discomfort.

When we're grateful for the years,
rather than fear them going by,
we enjoy life.

We are present in the now
knowing that is what we truly have –
the now.

When we look upon the past
with a grateful heart,

to the future
with excitement and to

the present moment
with curiosity
and all of our attention

we are free.

Sinking into life,
rather than reaching
beyond it.

Loving where I'm at,
loving who I am,
in the now.

At times there is
confusion in my mind.

I let the thoughts

come
and go

and I know

not everything
I think is true.

I move through emotions,
let myself feel them
and come back to
the stillness within.

I trust in God, in Jesus.

I am so grateful
to be held
in my humanness.

Lately I've been realizing
the conversations I will remember
when I'm 80 years old
won't be about me telling
my mother, my father,
those I love
about the success in my life
or how my dreams
are coming to fruition.

What I will remember
is the laughter my
mother and I share
talking about her day
or something she saw
on the Internet.

I will remember the
laughter my father and I
shared over the rare tuna
he ordered on a
sunny California pier
because he thought it
was hard to find,
not pink on the inside.

Lately I've been realizing
what is truly important is
not so much what you do,
rather, *who you are,*
what you notice,
& how you love.

Printed in the USA
CPSIA information can be obtained
at www.ICGtesting.com
CBHW012119291024
16599CB00060B/957